Gifted By Grace

An Introduction to the Holy Spirit and Spiritual Gifts

Study Guide

JEFF CARVER

Gifted by Grace: An Introduction to The Holy Spirit and Spiritual Gifts

Cover photo: John Maglica

ISBN: 1499126034
ISBN-13: 978-1499126037

DEDICATION

To my wife, Michelle, who always supports me in my relentless and wild pursuits of ministry. Without you I wouldn't have the focus and passion necessary to complete even a single task in service to our Lord and God Jesus Christ.

I love you always.

CONTENTS

ACKNOWLEDGMENTS

There are a few special people who have given their resources, time, energy, and encouragement to this study.

To each of you I am especially grateful.

Jeff Evans
Mindy Putnam
John Maglica
Dane Arsenault

LESSON 1: A NEW LIFE

It's always a good idea to start at the beginning. Or better said it is best to begin with the most important thing. In this study we are focusing on the Holy Spirit and spiritual gifts, but we first have to be sure that we center our hearts on the main thing: the gospel of Jesus Christ.

Briefly describe the gospel in your own words:

Read 1 Corinthians 15:1-4

In verse 3, the Apostle Paul describes the gospel as being of "first importance." Notice that he addresses those in Corinth who already have believed in the gospel and received it by faith. Paul emphasizes the importance of the gospel in Romans 1:11-15 as well. He writes to believers telling them that he longs to spiritually strengthen them and preach the gospel to them.

In addressing Christians in this way, Paul points out that the gospel is of first importance not only to those who have not yet believed, but to those who have believed as well.

List the major elements of the gospel described in 1 Corinthians 15:1-4:

Christ died for our sins. That is the good news. But before we receive good news, we must acknowledge the bad news: we have all offended God.

Read the following passages:

Isaiah 53:6
Romans 3:10-18
Romans 3:23
Romans 5:12-14
Romans 6:23
Ephesians 2:1-3
Ephesians 5:3-8
Colossians 3:5-10
Titus 3:3
James 2:10

What does the Bible say about the extent of sin in the human race?

What tendencies do we have toward God?

Describe some of the effects of our sin. What is the result (i.e. the wages) of sin?

We are all guilty before God. And the Bible says we are helpless to do anything about it. We deserve death. So what does this death look like?

Read the following verses:

Revelation 20:11-15
Revelation 21:8

Physical death is the cessation of life and the separation of our immaterial self (i.e. soul, spirit) from our bodies. The second death, or eternal death, is the separation of our souls from the presence of God for eternity. The Bible describes eternal death in terrifying terms of physical and spiritual anguish.

We cannot atone for our own rebellion and guilt and thus we cannot, on our own power, avoid the death we deserve. We need to be rescued. We need a Savior.

So God provided a way.

Read the following passages:

Matthew 20:28
John 1:29
John 3:16-21
Romans 3:23-26
Romans 5:6-8
Galatians 1:3-5
1 Peter 2:22-24
1 Peter 3:18

How is the work of Jesus described in these verses?

What are the results of the sacrifice of Jesus on the cross?

How is God the Father involved in Jesus' sacrifice?

Jesus absorbed the wrath of God the Father for our sins. He took the punishment we deserved upon Himself so that we could spend eternity with Him in heaven. This is an astonishing and nearly incomprehensible truth. That He would humble Himself and die for your sin and my sin reveals His inexhaustible grace and love for us. We are ransomed and rescued by Jesus so we do not have to face the wrath of God the Father for eternity.

But the work of Jesus on the cross doesn't end in the grave. The Bible says that He rose again on the third day.

Read the following passages:

Matthew 16:21
Matthew 20:18-19
Matthew 28:1-6
John 10:18
Acts 2:23-24, 32
Acts 13:30
Acts 17:31
Romans 6:4
Romans 8:11
1 Corinthians 15:4
1 Corinthians 6:14
Colossians 2:10

From these verses we see that God the Father (Acts 2:32), Jesus (John 10:18), and the Holy Spirit (Romans 8:11) are unified in action in the resurrection of Jesus Christ from the dead.

In John 14:19 Jesus says, "Because I live, you also will live." This is an amazing promise and is the hope of all who believe in Him for salvation. When we die, we will live. We will live because Jesus overcame the grave and He promises we will do the same in victory.

Paul reflects on the resurrection body and the victory that we have in Jesus over death in 1 Corinthians 15:35-58. Take some time to read this passage and reflect on its meaning and the hope that is offered to all who believe in Christ for salvation.

What to do now?

If you have not placed your faith in Jesus Christ for salvation, then today is the day to do it. Now is the time of salvation (2 Corinthians 6:2) and today is the day for you to be reconciled to God through Jesus. There is no reason to put it off any longer. He will forgive you of all of your sins, past, present, and future. Psalm 103:12 says, "as far as the east is from the west, so far does he remove our transgressions from us."

The Lord will give you new life as He promised and will receive you as His own child (John 1:12; Romans 8:16-17). You will no longer be under the wrath of God, and even your troubles will be caused to work out for your good (1 Thessalonians 5:9-10; Romans 8:28). Life on earth will still not be perfect, but you will have a perfect Savior to walk through it with you day by day.

For those who have Jesus as their Lord and Savior, He challenges you to stand firm in the faith and walk steadily in it.

Read Romans 1:16 and 1 Corinthians 1:18

What is the gospel to the believer?

Why should you saturate your life with the hearing and reading of the gospel?

Read the following passages:

1 Corinthians 15:58
Ephesians 2:8-10
Colossians 1:9-14

All Christians have work to do. We do not work for our salvation, but we do work because of it. We work in response to the sacrifice that Jesus has made on our behalf, the sacrifice of His own life that has given us new life. We were created "for good works" that have been prepared for us so we can bring glory to God.

What work do you believe God has prepared for you to do?

What is holding you back?

Questions for Group Discussion

How would you explain the gospel to someone who has never heard it?

Why is the resurrection an important part of the gospel?

How has the gospel personally affected your life and the way you live?

Why is it important to be able to understand and explain the gospel as a Christian?

What are some benefits of "preaching the gospel to yourself?"

If you are a believer, briefly share your personal testimony of salvation.

How can you share the gospel and your testimony with someone this week?

LESSON 2: WHO IS THE HOLY SPIRIT?

God has not revealed everything about Himself to mankind. As finite creatures, we are limited in our ability to comprehend and receive revelation from the Lord. He knows this and has designed us in such a way that we desire more than we can take in. The doctrine of the Trinity is a perfect example of this. God has revealed Himself in Scripture as a Triune God. One God, three Persons: Father, Son, and Holy Spirit. This may be the most difficult doctrine for our human minds to comprehend. However, we accept it as true because we trust that God has given us the Scriptures and they reveal the true nature of God to us.

The Father has also given us all that we need to understand how we are to respond in worship and in faith toward His Son Jesus Christ. His Holy Spirit is the One who by grace gives us new hearts that love and long for The Lord. These new hearts can do nothing but respond in faith to the salvation that Jesus has purchased for us. With the Father, Son and Holy Spirit we have all we need to live a godly and worshipful life.

The Holy Spirit is possibly the least understood Person in the Triune Godhead. When we study the Holy Spirit we must begin by acknowledging our inability to take hold of Him and comprehend Him fully. This does not mean we cannot know Him. We can know Him in terms of our relationship with Him and we can know His will and direction for our lives. What we cannot know usually corresponds to our questions of "how" or "why" He does one thing or another. It's not that He wants to keep us in the dark, it's just that some things are meant to be revealed and others are not. We see this in interactions between Jesus and His disciples as well. God has ways and plans and purposes that are above our own and He asks us to trust in that on a daily basis. He is sovereign and good.

Read Exodus 33:12-23

What did Moses want from God?

In verse 12:

In verse 13:

In verses 15-16:

In the same way the activities of God the Father are often unseen, the activities of God the Holy Spirit are also unseen. This is revealed in His work in salvation.

Read John 3:1-8

What does it mean to be born again?

Read John 1:12-13

Compare this passage with John 3:5-7. Who is responsible for salvation? (By whose will are people saved?)

How is the Holy Spirit like the wind?

We don't know how the Holy Spirit changes a person's heart, but we know that He does. Give a few examples of the effects of the Holy Spirit's work which are visible and prove His transforming power.

We see that the Holy Spirit is mysterious, but God has revealed what we need to know about Him in the Scriptures. We already see some characteristics of the Holy Spirit in Jesus' description in the gospel of John. These characteristics reveal that the Holy Spirit is not a mere force or power, but He is a person.

Read the following verses:

2 Samuel 23:2
Isaiah 63:10
John 14:26
John 16:13-14
Acts 13:2
Romans 8:16, 26-27
Romans 15:30
Ephesians 4:30
Philippians 1:19
1 Thessalonians 5:19

The Holy Spirit is described in various ways in these passages. List the different attributes of His personhood which are revealed.

Now that we have established the personhood of the Holy Spirit, we must ask the next logical question: Who is He? What is His identity? Again we will go to the Scriptures for our answer.

Read the following passages:

Matthew 28:19
1 Corinthians 12:4-6
2 Corinthians 13:14
Ephesians 4:4-6
1 Peter 1:2
Jude 20-21

These passages are often called "Trinitarian verses." In them The Holy Spirit is revealed as having equal stature with God the Father and God the Son. He is treated as God and given reverence as God. Just as the Holy Spirit has the attributes of personhood, He possesses the attributes of deity as well.

Read the following verses:

Genesis 1:2
Psalm 139:7-8
Acts 5:3-4
Romans 8:11
1 Corinthians 2:10-11
Hebrews 9:14

List the attributes of deity the Holy Spirit possesses.

In Genesis 1:2 we see the Holy Spirit present at the creation of the earth. The earth at this point is dark and void and unable to sustain life. This of course is not a problem for God who brings life out of nothing, and does this by His Holy Spirit. The Holy Spirit is often referred to as the "Life-Giver."

In Genesis 2:7 we read that God breathed life into the nostrils of Adam whom He formed from the dust. The imagery here is that of the Holy Spirit animating and giving physical life to man.

Read the following passages:

Job 27:3-4
Job 33:4
Ezekiel 37:8-10

The Spirit is intimately involved in giving us physical life but that's not all. We have already read John 3:1-8 which reveals the Spirit's work in giving us new life in Jesus Christ. The Holy Spirit has a ministry of regeneration. He changes hearts, bringing them to know and follow Jesus. He brings new life to those who were once "dead in their sins," (Ephesians 2:1) and who were under the wrath of God (John 3:36).

Read the following verses:

Ezekiel 37:14
Joel 2:28
John 6:63
John 7:38-39
Acts 2:33
Acts 10:45
Romans 8:2
1 Corinthians 6:11
2 Corinthians 3:5-6
Titus 3:5-6

What does God promise believers regarding His Holy Spirit?

What are the results and benefits of the new life given to us through the Spirit?

The Bible says the Holy Spirit is "poured out" several times in these verses. What does this imagery say about God the Father? What does it imply or reveal about the Holy Spirit?

How does the new life we are given change our standing before God the Father? How are we changed in the process?

The Holy Spirit is intimately involved in giving us physical life, new life in Jesus, and finally a glorified life in eternity. Jesus said in John 10:27-28, "My sheep hear my voice, and I know them, and they follow me. I give them eternal life, and they will never perish, and no one will snatch them out of my hand."

Jesus promises that those who believe in Him for salvation will never perish. Their eternal place in heaven is guaranteed by the Holy Spirit who dwells in them. And their glorification, being given new, imperishable, eternally glorified bodies, is carried out by the Holy Spirit.

Read the following verses:

Romans 8:11
Romans 8:30
2 Corinthians 5:1-5
Ephesians 1:13-14

Many people suffer from physical ailments and limitations. As we age, we all begin to feel the weight of this in our lives. Our bodies begin to slowly betray and fail us and we realize we aren't invincible anymore. It becomes evident that these bodies were not made to last forever.

In 2 Corinthians 5:1-5, Paul emphasizes this struggle in every person's life. He likens our physical bodies on earth to "tents" and reveals our heavenly bodies will be like "buildings."

How are our earthly, physical bodies like "tents?"

What will change when you inherit a new "building from God?"

What do you look forward to the most about having a new glorified body?

The mystery of the Holy Spirit is profound, but much has been revealed in the Scriptures about Him and His ministry on earth. He is "the One who gives life" and who dwells in us and fills us with His holy presence and power.

He loves us just as the Father and Son love us. We are called to have a present and intimate relationship with Him and to yield to His holy will and direction for our lives. He is deeply connected to us and profoundly concerned with our spiritual walk.

Questions for Group Discussion

The apparent mysteriousness of the Holy Spirit often hinders people from even attempting to understand Him and His ministry. Share your thoughts on the Holy Spirit and how you might grow in your relationship with Him.

Why is it important to understand that the Holy Spirit has personhood and is not a mere "force" or power?

How does recognizing the personhood of the Holy Spirit help you to connect with Him? How does knowing that you can lie to the Holy Spirit or grieve Him affect your interaction with Him?

Read John 14:26, 15:26, and 16:7. The Scriptures reveal that the Holy Spirit is God and He is sent by, or proceeds from, both the Father and the Son. What does this reveal about the Holy Spirit and His role in the Trinity?

Read John 6:63. How does this verse challenge your thoughts as to your level of involvement in your own salvation? How does it help solidify the role and the place of the Spirit in your life?

Knowing that the Holy Spirit is intimately involved in giving you life (physical life, a new regenerated life, and an eternal glorified life), how can you respond in your relationship with Him?

The Holy Spirit loves you just as the Father and the Son love you. How does the love of God affect your daily walk with Him? How will you reveal that love to others in your circle of influence?

LESSON 3: WALK BY THE SPIRIT

Grace is something that baffles the human heart. We often are unwilling or don't know how to give it, and we have an even more difficult time receiving it. We like merit. We like to earn the approval of others and we expect others to earn our approval. It is a perfectly fair system and we tend to think that we can thrive in it. Of course the truth is that we all fail and, if we are honest, we judge the failures of our neighbors more harshly than our own. So having a human heart makes true fairness unattainable.

But God is different. He doesn't play fair. Don't get this wrong, He is perfectly just in everything He does, but He has a different view of fairness. He doesn't play fair because that would make our relationship with Him impossible. Have you ever had a relationship where you each played fairly no matter what? Every time you hurt them, they hurt you in return? And they only treated you well when they were being treated well? Relationships like that never last.

This is particularly true in marriage. It's not about playing fair, but about "out-loving" each other. The Bible tells us to "outdo one another in showing honor" (Romans 12:10) and to humbly "count others as more significant than yourselves."

(Philippians 2:3) Humility in love is the key to a strong and lasting relationship. Grace is the result of that humility and love.

God doesn't treat us how we have treated Him. Instead He gives grace. He pours out grace abundantly over us. His grace is the reason we have new life in Jesus. The Holy Spirit is the One who applies that grace to our hearts and comes to dwell in us. He dwells in us as our seal and guarantee of eternal life.

Read the following verses:

2 Corinthians 1:22
2 Corinthians 5:5
Ephesians 1:13-14

The Holy Spirit is the proof of God's grace over us and in us. Knowing this truth should give us confidence in the work that The Lord has accomplished on our behalf. Our assurance in Him and in the work He has done allows us to walk in confidence in the work He has prepared for us to do. What other reasons do you think God wants us to have this confidence?

Galatians 5:25 says, "If we live by the Spirit, let us also walk by the Spirit." What does this mean?

We live by the Spirit, and because the Spirit is the applier of grace we can also say, "We live by grace." We have breath because of God's grace. We have life because of God's grace.

Read Ephesians 2:8-9

We are saved by grace, based on no work of our own but solely on the work of Jesus Christ on the cross. So if we are saved by grace, how can we then live out the rest of our lives apart from that grace on our own power? It is impossible. We do not have the ability or strength in and of ourselves to live the life He has for us. We need His grace.

So when Paul says, "If we live by the Spirit, let us also walk by the Spirit," he is instructing us to rely on the same grace that gave us eternal life to sustain and empower our daily walk here on this earth.

Read Galatians 3:1-3

What is Paul's argument in verse 3?

Here Paul is confronting a problem all Christians face in their walk with Jesus: self-reliance. At a certain point in our Christian lives we begin to think that we have it all together, or we at least can handle some things on our own. The Galatians' issue was with the Law of Moses. They wanted to return to the old way of doing things thinking that would somehow please God. The problem with their thinking is that wasn't the purpose of the Law. The Law was meant to reveal the need for a Savior and to point to the truth that works don't please God, faith alone does.

We have a human tendency to be self-reliant. We want to work for what we have. The root of this thinking is pride. We want to prove our worth. We want to show that we deserve what we get, even salvation. Often we don't realize it or we won't admit it, but this attitude is actually a rejection of Jesus' sacrifice on the cross. It is also a rejection of the Spirit who is working in us.

In what ways are you self-reliant? What areas of your life are you relying too much on your own strength or wisdom?

Why do you think these things are so difficult to give to The Lord?

What is the result of holding on so tightly and working so hard on your own?

The Holy Spirit is at work in you, guiding you, empowering you, and helping you to grow and look more like Jesus every day. This is a process for each Christian. The word used in Scripture for this is sanctification. There are different categories or phases of sanctification. The first is that of "being set apart for holy use." This begins at salvation.

Read the following verses:

Acts 20:32
1 Corinthians 6:11

These verses illustrate the initial break from the old life of sin and its grip on our hearts. Read all of Romans chapter 6 and reflect on the new condition and standing of the believer in relation to Christ and also to sin.

In verses 1-11, what is our new standing with Christ?

What is our standing in regard to sin?

Although we have been freed from the punishment of our sin and the power of sin, we are not yet free from the presence of it. We still battle each day with temptation and the draw of sin. The second phase of sanctification is that of being made more and more like Jesus and conforming to His image and will for our lives. It is growing in Christlikeness.

In Romans 6 Paul puts forth the truth that we are freed from the power and punishment of sin, but he also recognizes that there is a remnant of it in our hearts.

From verses 12-14, how are we to deal with sin?

The principle of replacing sin with righteousness is declared in other passages of Scripture.

Read the following passages:

Luke 11:24-26
Ephesians 4:20-32

Sanctification is not merely the process of emptying your heart and life of sin, it is also the filling of your heart and life with righteousness by grace. Many people want to "clean up their lives," but they use their own filthy rags to do it.

In the Luke 11 passage above, the person who the demon left got their life straightened out and tidied up, but they were still empty, waiting for something to fill them again. Instead of being indwelt by the Holy Spirit, they left the door open to more demons. Human beings will fill their hearts with sin or they will be filled by grace with righteousness through the Holy Spirit. That is the major point of the Ephesians 4 passage as well as Romans 6.

The amazing thing about this is that we are called to participate in our own sanctification with the Holy Spirit.

Read 2 Peter 1:3-11

What is the source of all we need to live a godly life?

What is the promise of living this kind of life?

Notice the order of this passage. In verse 5 it says, "For this very reason, make every effort to…" We are able to live godly lives because of what God has given us. In addition to that, we live in response to what He has done by His grace, not in order to gain His favor. Our lives are a reflection of and a response to God's loving and powerful work in us.

Not only do we need God's grace to become the people He desires us to be, we need His grace to live out the mission He has called us to fulfill. This includes both the Greatest Commandment and the Great Commission.

Read the following passages:

Mark 12:28-31
Matthew 28:18-20

We cannot do this on our own power. In fact, we don't want to do this apart from the call of God on our lives and the moving of the Holy Spirit in our hearts. Thankfully Jesus has promised to be with us always for that mission, and He has given us His Holy Spirit to empower and guide us.

Read John 15:1-11

In this passage Jesus gives us a vision of what our life is to be like in Him. He is the Vine, we are the branches. We have been grafted into the Vine by the Vinedresser, who is God the Father. The life-giving sap that flows from the Vine to the branch is the Holy Spirit.

In verse 5 Jesus said, "apart from me you can do nothing." We cannot bear fruit apart from Jesus and the sap of the Holy Spirit. A branch that is not connected to the Vine is only good for firewood. But a branch connected to the Vine, receiving nutrients through the sap, bears much fruit and brings glory to the Vinedresser. Much fruit shows the care and expertise of the Vinedresser. It reveals His passion and the time He has taken to make it what it is and get the most out of it.

The branch is powerless but for the Vine. It has no life apart from the Vine. It has no useful purpose apart from the Vine except to be burned up. Only as it remains connected to the Vine does it fulfill its true and intended purpose: to bear much fruit.

Read 1 Peter 4:7-11

We are stewards of God's grace, using His power to do His will for His glory.

The final phase of sanctification comes when we enter the kingdom of God forever. We are perfected by His grace and will finally be freed from the presence of sin. The result of our being set apart for holy use and being conformed to the image of Christ during our life here on earth is the revelation of the glory of God to all. Our final sanctification is meant to glorify God in eternity.

"If we live by the Spirit, let us also walk by the Spirit." We have received His grace for life. Let us now walk by that same grace in this life and toward our promised eternal life.

Questions for Group Discussion

Briefly describe grace in your own terms.

Why do you think it is so difficult to receive grace?

How might your own self-reliance be holding you back from the life and ministry The Lord has for you?

Discuss the Greatest Commandment. What are some ways you are loving God and your neighbor in His power? What are some practical outcomes of loving God and others?

The Great Commission is meant for every Christian to fulfill. The "much fruit" in John 15:8 refers mainly to the salvation of souls. What is our responsibility when it comes to another person's salvation?

What are some ways you can help other believers "walk by the Spirit?"

Jesus said in John 15:5, "I am the vine; you are the branches. Whoever abides in me and I in him, he it is that bears much fruit, for apart from me you can do nothing." How can we abide in Christ more fully and continually? Share some ways you have been able to stay connected to Him daily.

LESSON 4: WHAT ARE SPIRITUAL GIFTS?

Who doesn't love to receive a gift? No matter the occasion or even the lack of an occasion, we all love gifts. A gift is an expression of the giver's love and appreciation for the one who is receiving it. Gifts are meant to reveal the giver's heart and display it to the recipient. The gift itself is not only to be a symbol of love and appreciation, but it is to be received and enjoyed.

The same is true of spiritual gifts, but to a higher degree. Spiritual gifts are from God and are given as a symbol of His divine grace and love for His people. They are meant to be received and used for His glory and in fulfillment of His perfect will. So what is a spiritual gift? How are spiritual gifts to be understood by Christians?

The definition we will use for this study is this: **A spiritual gift is a supernatural ability given to believers in Jesus, who have received the Holy Spirit, to do ministry for God in His Kingdom.**

There are two Greek words in the New Testament that are translated "spiritual gifts." The first is *pneumatikon*, which has as its root the word *pneuma*, meaning "spirit." The second is *charisma* which comes from the root word *charis*, meaning "grace." Each of these words tells us something about spiritual gifts.

Pneumatikon signifies that the gifts are of the Holy Spirit. They are an expression of His power, love and divine will through the individual in the context of the church. Like the wind they may not always be visible, but their effects are evident. They are animated and empowered as the will of the Spirit of God moves.

The word charisma indicates that spiritual gifts are measures of grace given by The Lord. In fact, they are sometimes referred to as "grace gifts." These charismata are given to those who have already received saving grace from God through faith in Jesus Christ. As we learned in the previous lesson, The Lord gives us everything we need to live a godly life. By giving spiritual gifts to His church as an extra measure of grace, He ensures that it is well-equipped to build itself up in love and accomplish His mission on earth.

Read Ephesians 4:11-16

This passage contains one of the three main lists of gifts found in Scripture. Which gifts are listed?

There are at least eight direct results and benefits for the church that come from these gifts. List as many as you can below.

Spiritual gifts are supernatural. This means that they are outside of the realm of nature. They cannot be explained by natural law and are not able to be obtained or learned by natural means. They can only be explained as supernaturally coming from God according to His will.

Special talent or aptitude is also a gift from God. Everyone has some sort of gift, ability or aptitude that they are given seemingly at birth. This is evidence of God's common grace to all of mankind. Every human is made in God's image and all have some aspects of giftedness that reflect the image of their Creator. Both spiritual gifts and talents have their origin in God, however, there are significant differences between the two.

God allows talents to be used for our own purposes. We see this everywhere we look: in every business we visit, in every movie we watch and every song we hear. People everywhere use their talents for their own benefits and rewards. This is not necessarily an issue since everyone needs to make a living, but it becomes a problem when we use our abilities solely for our own profit.

Read the following verses:

1 Corinthians 10:31
Colossians 3:17

The problem with using our talents and abilities solely for our own benefit is that God is not glorified in them.

When it comes to spiritual gifts, God opens up the opportunity for His people to serve Him and bring Him glory in those gifts. Only Christians are given spiritual gifts, so only they can bring God glory in exercising them. The unbeliever cannot please God or bring Him glory in his own talents. There is no opportunity for them to bring Him glory outside of a relationship with His Son Jesus Christ.

Although talents and spiritual gifts are all given by God, talents lack one other thing: they do not have a supernatural effect in the world. Spiritual gifts have their source in God and their effect is supernatural. This is true even in the outwardly *normal* or *ordinary* types of gifts. Hearts being transformed by spoken words, or mercy that draws the brokenhearted to Jesus are supernatural results. Healing and faith and worship that come as a result of being faithful stewards of our spiritual gifts are expressly supernatural outcomes.

The joy that comes from this faithfulness is unsurpassed. God is gracious in giving us joy and satisfaction in the work done in His power and in His name.

We have already touched on the fact that spiritual gifts are from God, but it will benefit us to expand on this truth. In the Scriptures we read that since the day of Pentecost the Holy Spirit has given gifts to the church.

Read the following verses:

Acts 1:4-8
Acts 2:1-21
Ephesians 4:7-13
1 Corinthians 12:1-11
Hebrews 2:4

What did Jesus promise in Acts 1:8?

What was the result of the Holy Spirit coming over the church in Acts 2:1-4?

How did the crowd react in Acts 2:5-13?

In your experience, how do people react to the movement of the Holy Spirit today?

In 1 Corinthians 12:4-11, how is each Person in the Trinity involved in the giving and empowering of spiritual gifts?

We see God the Father, God the Son and God the Holy Spirit are all intimately involved with distributing, empowering and animating spiritual gifts in the individual believer in the context of the church body.

This brings us to another point: spiritual gifts are to be used in ministry in unity and connection with other believers. This is God's purpose and design for spiritual gifts. Christians must be sure to remember that God's will supersedes our own. We should never try to use our gifts for our own purposes or in our own power. As soon as we attempt to do this, we will not only fail to bring God glory, we will invite His holy discipline on our lives.

Read 2 Corinthians 4:7

What treasure is Paul speaking of in this verse?

What does it mean that we are jars of clay?

Read 2 Corinthians 4:8-15

Is this a hopeful passage? Why or why not?

List the many reasons Paul gives for continuing on in his ministry.

God knows that He places perfect gifts into the hands of imperfect people. We make mistakes and we fall short of His intentions all the time. We will continue fail to use our gifts or use them properly. But He is gracious and loving to forgive us and help us grow in these things. He has always used people with pasts and history, but this is how He gets the glory. His grace is on full display when He uses us.

Questions for Group Discussion

What is the best gift you have ever received? Who gave it to you? Why was it so special to you? What is the best gift you have ever given? Who did you give it to and why?

Read Ephesians 4:11-12. What is the significance of the spiritual gifts that are listed? How are these gifts foundational to the church?

Discuss the difference between talents and spiritual gifts. If you could have any talent or spiritual gift what would it be? Why?

Why is it important that the Father, Son, and Holy Spirit are each involved in the giving and empowering of spiritual gifts? What does this say about the importance of gifts in the life of the individual believer and in the church?

What is the danger of exercising spiritual gifts in our own power?

Knowing the gifts that are seemingly ordinary are actually supernatural in their origin and in their effect, how should this affect your view of those gifts?

God puts His perfect gifts and the treasure of His gospel into jars of clay. Why do you think He entrusts us with these things? What does this reveal about God? What can you do to be a good steward of the gospel and the spiritual gift(s) God has given you?

LESSON 5: THE PURPOSE OF SPIRITUAL GIFTS

Everything has a purpose. Everyone has a purpose. Every purpose of everything and everyone who ever existed has its origin in the perfect plan, the perfect will and the perfect heart of God. He is sovereign and good and His purposes are holy and high.

Those purposes are often not understood by the people He created. We do not have the benefit of knowing everything and seeing how all of creation and history and future fit together. We are limited in our understanding of life and in our ability to see beyond our own circumstances. Certainly Job did not understand what God was up to when he was in the midst of his suffering. Noah probably had some questions when God told him to build an ark. Abraham had no clue what God had planned for him and his (not yet existent) offspring when He was told to leave everything and go to a foreign land. This is a theme throughout the Scriptures and throughout our personal human experience with God.

Jesus came to live amongst His creation and His purpose was often misunderstood by His followers. His disciples, who were intimately connected to Him and learning from Him every day, did not fully understand His purpose or mission until after He ascended to Heaven.

Read the following verses.

John 12:16
John 13:7
John 16:16-18
John 20:8-10
Mark 9:30-32
Luke 17:20-21
Luke 19:11
Acts 1:6

The disciples couldn't understand why Jesus did not set up His kingdom after His resurrection. They figured this was the time to overthrow the Romans and establish the earthly rule of God forever. But Jesus knew The Father's purposes were not fulfilled yet. It was now time for the Holy Spirit to be sent to complete the purpose of God on earth.

Just think: Jesus had you and me in mind here. He was thinking of all of the future generations of faithful believers that would be saved by His great sacrifice on the cross, and His overcoming death in His resurrection. His heart was on all those who would believe in Him and be saved by grace through faith placed in Him.

Read John 16:5-7

Jesus said that He needed to leave, but it was to the disciples' advantage that He did. Think of how difficult that message would have been to receive. They would have been in disbelief. Jesus had just conquered death and it seemed to them the perfect time to set up His own kingdom. How could He leave now? Where was He going? What was the meaning of all of this?

They were being forced to trust that Jesus knew what was best in God's perfect plan. Graciously He did not leave them, or us, as orphans. He said it would be to our advantage that He go away so He could send the Holy Spirit. We have the benefit of hindsight, so what does this tell us about the Holy Spirit's ministry?

In your own words, describe the purpose of the Holy Spirit's ministry on earth today.

To know the purpose of spiritual gifts, we must first understand the purpose of the Holy Spirit here on earth. There are many reasons why the Father and Son sent the Holy Spirit. You can see several of them by studying the different names of the Holy Spirit found in Scripture.

Read the following verses:

John 14:16-17, 26
John 16:13
Romans 1:4
Romans 8:2, 14-16
2 Corinthians 4:13
Ephesians 1:17
Hebrews 10:29
1 Peter 4:14

These names and descriptions of the Holy Spirit reveal many aspects of His purpose and mission on this earth. But the primary purpose we find is that of the Spirit of Glory described in 1 Peter 4:14. He has come to glorify, to bring glory and to reveal glory.

Read John 15:26 and John 16:13-15

Just as Jesus brought glory to The Father in His earthly ministry (John 14:13; 17:1, 4), the Holy Spirit's purpose is to bring glory to Jesus in His ministry. Jesus said in John 16:14 that the Holy Spirit "will bring Me glory." So how does He do this?

If we look at these two passages we see that the Holy Spirit does two things to bring Jesus glory.

First, He testifies, or bears witness, about Jesus. This is very clear in John 15:26, and if we look closely we see the same thing in John 16:13-15. Here He reveals the glory of Jesus to His people. Jesus says, "He will take what is mine and declare it to you." What Jesus has is "all that the Father has." What the Father has He has given to the Son. And what is that? It is authority and honor.

Read John 5:19-29

The Holy Spirit bears witness about Jesus and reveals His glory. We see in the New Testament that He has already done this in Jesus' earthly life.

Read the following verses:

Luke 1:67-70
Matthew 3:16-17
Romans 1:1-4

In these verses we see that the Holy Spirit testified of Jesus' glory before His birth, at His baptism, and in His resurrection. Today the Holy Spirit continues testifying of the glory of Jesus through the gospel. He gifts men and women to share the gospel with others. Whenever and wherever the gospel is preached, the Holy Spirit is at work in the hearts of God's people. Yes, they are God's people even before they know it or receive the right to become "sons of God" (John 1:12). The Holy Spirit testifies of Jesus' glory directly to the hearts of the lost to bring them into the family of God as adopted children.

Not only does the Holy Spirit glorify Jesus by testifying of Him, but He glorifies Jesus through the building up of His church. In John 16:13 we see that the Holy Spirit, The Spirit of Truth, would "guide them into all truth." This is the foundational work of building up of the Body of Christ.

Jesus said He would build His church (Matthew 16:18) and a major way that He accomplishes this is by sending His Holy Spirit to gift the church, empower the church, and unify the church so that it builds itself up in love.

Read Ephesians 4:4-16

If the mission and purpose of the Holy Spirit is to glorify Jesus by testifying of Him and building up His church, what conclusion must we come to about the purpose of spiritual gifts? Their purpose must be the same as the Holy Spirit who gives them: *to glorify Jesus by testifying of Him and edifying His church.*

First, we will testify of Jesus.

Read the following verses:

John 15:26-27
Acts 1:8
1 John 1:1-2; 4:14

We are called to bear witness to the glory of Jesus. We can only do this if we know the truth. If we know the truth it will flow out from our hearts into our speech and our lives. We speak the truth and we live the truth. Both of these things must work in harmony. Speaking the truth without living it is called hypocrisy. Living the truth without speaking it is called cowardice. We fail to glorify Jesus if we do not live and speak the truth in love to the world.

Which of these would you say you have the most difficulty with, speaking the truth or living the truth? What about doing these things in love?

What opportunities can you identify in your life where you can witness to the glory of Jesus? Where have you been timid or even fearful in fulfilling your purpose in this area?

Jesus is gracious and wants to see you fully experiencing the joy of sharing and living the truth of His love and grace. He is glorified in these things. The Father is glorified in these things. These things result in much fruit. This is why He sent His Holy Spirit to guide and direct you. He loves you and wants an abundant life for you. Not a life of accumulating and receiving as much as you can from this world, but life of bearing an abundance of fruit in His name.

Read John 15:8

Proving that we are disciples by bearing much fruit brings glory to God the Father. This also brings glory to Jesus.

Not only do we witness to the glory of Jesus, but we are called and commanded to build up His church in love in our daily walk and service to Him.

Read the following verses:

1 Corinthians 12:7
1 Corinthians 14:12, 26
1 Peter 4:10

We are to build one another up in the church in the name of Jesus for His glory and for our benefit. A principal way we do this is through exercising our spiritual gifts in the power of the Holy Spirit, in love and humility, honoring one another above ourselves (Romans 12:10, Philippians 2:3).

Jesus loves His bride, the Church. We are that Bride and we are to love one another. This can be difficult as we are all different and each of us has shortcomings and remaining sin that hinders us in our relationships with one another. This is why forgiveness is so important in the church. Every one of us needs it and every one of us needs to extend it to others. As Christ forgave, so should we forgive. As He loved, so should we love.

God has given us every gift we need to be able to build up the church in love. We lack nothing to be able to live out the mission of Jesus on earth and glorify Him in our lives. So whether you are an apostle, a prophet, a teacher, an encourager, a giver, a server, or whatever you are, you are a part of the body of Christ and you are called to build up the rest of the body in love.

Read Ephesians 4:15-16

Christ has given us His life by His grace and this new life is to have purpose in Him. That purpose is to glorify Him and build up His church in love until He returns. He has given us His Spirit who gives us gifts to fulfill that purpose.

Questions for Group Discussion

Before you became a Christian, did you have a sense of purpose? What did you feel your purpose was in this life? How has that changed or developed?

Read Romans 8:18-39. How does knowing that God has a plan and a purpose for everything, everyone, and every circumstance affect how you approach life? How does this passage put into perspective the difficult and sometimes terrible trials we experience? What is the final conclusion of these verses?

Compare Romans 8:29 with 1 Corinthians 15:49. How do these verses connect to your ultimate purpose of glorifying The Lord?

How do you see the Holy Spirit bringing glory to Jesus in the church today?

Why is it important to know the true purpose of spiritual gifts? Did you have a different view of their purpose before this lesson?

How does the exercising of our spiritual gifts build the church up? Why should we strive to build up the church?

Serving in our spiritual gifts gives us opportunities to speak and live out the truth in love. What are some ways you can do this in your daily life? In what ways are you succeeding in this now? How can you "tune in" to the Holy Spirit more deeply to hear His will and promptings each day?

LESSON 6: DISCOVER YOUR SPIRITUAL GIFT

The purpose of the Holy Spirit is to glorify Jesus. That's the purpose of every Christian as well. If you love Him, you will seek to serve and honor Him in all that you do. A major way we serve and honor Jesus is in the exercising of our spiritual gifts.

In the previous lessons we learned that God loves us and wants us to be a part of His family as adopted children. He sent His own Son Jesus to die for our sins and take the wrath of The Father on the cross. This wrath was meant for all of us because we've all sinned against our holy and perfect God. Because Jesus died this death and rose again, if we put our faith in what He has done, we will have eternal life with Him in heaven. What great love He has for us to take our sin and give us His righteousness! And we did nothing to deserve it! This is true grace.

Not only has He given us much grace, He has also given us His Spirit as a guarantee of our belonging to Him, to dwell with us and in us. The Spirit loves us just as Jesus and The Father love us. He abides intimately with us to guide and empower our daily walk with Jesus. He is a good and gracious God.

We have learned that The Spirit of God is God. God exists in Trinity. He is Father, Son, and Holy Spirit: three unique Persons yet one God. This mystery is perfect and profound. It isn't meant to hinder us but to drive us deeper into communion with Him.

Just as we were saved by the grace of this amazing God, we are called to walk by that same grace. "If we live by the Spirit, let us also walk by the Spirit" means to walk by the grace He pours out each day. It means to walk in the life that He gives each moment, and to follow His lead in every aspect of our lives.

The Spirit gives us life and He adds purpose and power to that life. One way He does this is by giving us spiritual gifts. These are supernaturally given and the effects of their proper use are supernatural as well.

We have learned that spiritual gifts are special abilities that all Christians are given for the glory of Jesus and the building up of His church in love. This is a holy purpose. In order to fulfill that purpose, you must know what gift or gifts you have. So how do you discover your spiritual gift? There are some simple steps you can take.

The first step is prayer.

Take a moment (or as long as you need) right now to pray. Praise God and thank Him for who He is and all He has done. Then simply ask Him to reveal what spiritual gift He has given you for His glory. Listen intently with your heart and ask Him to bless you with understanding and wisdom.

Write down anything that He reveals to you.

The next step is to read the Scriptures and see what The Lord reveals to you both about Himself and about yourself.

Read the following passages:

Romans 12:1-8
1 Corinthians 12:1-11, 27-31
Ephesians 4:11

List all of the spiritual gifts found in these three passages.

Which of these gifts stands out to you as something God may have given you?

A spiritual gift can spring from a natural talent, or it can be a completely new ability that is "out of the ordinary" for that person. Is this gift unusual for you or is it something that comes more naturally to you?

Many of the gifts listed in the Bible are not specifically defined or explained to us. How we deal with that is pretty basic: we look at the words themselves and figure out what they mean, and we look at the context in which they are used. For instance the Greek word for the spiritual gift of leadership is *proistemi*, and it means to lead, assist, protect and care for others. There are clues as to its meaning when we look at its use in various passages of Scripture. In 1 Timothy 3:5 Paul connects the gift of leadership to caring for others when he asks, "If someone does not know how to manage (*proistemi*) his own household, how will he care for God's church?" So we see that someone with the gift of leadership will likely exhibit various characteristics similar to those of a parent who leads and cares for their family.

This is just one short example of how we can learn about spiritual gifts in Scripture.

Take time now to go to **Appendix A** and read the descriptions of each spiritual gift. While you are reading, listen to any key words that may pop up and remind you of your own abilities or characteristics. Feel free to highlight and/or write your thoughts in the margins.

Another potential step in learning your spiritual gift is to look at various characters in the Bible, particularly those who are described or shown in the church age, essentially from the Book of Acts forward. When you study, pay special attention to the people and their unique characteristics and determine if you share any of those traits. You can also do this with people you currently know who are serving Jesus in their gifts. Who in the church shares your abilities? Who has similar passions and a heart for others? Who is easy to communicate with and relate to in your church? It may be those who have a similar spiritual gift.

Identifying others who are gifted in various ways, then comparing yourself to them can be helpful, but also problematic. Beware of thinking that you do not have a certain gift because you are not currently bearing as much fruit with that gift as someone else. Just because you do not have an international evangelistic ministry does not mean you do not have the gift of evangelism. It just means God is using you in different ways and to different degrees at this time. We need to recognize that we grow in our gifts throughout our lives as we grow in our obedience to serve in them. We are not to compare our fruit to others. Fruit is not dependent upon our efforts, but on the Holy Spirit. All we are called to do is abide in Christ, love God and our neighbors, and faithfully serve Him in our gifts.

The next thing you can do to discover your spiritual gift is to take a simple spiritual gifts test. A spiritual gifts test is not a guaranteed way to discover your spiritual gift, but it does serve as a guide to direct you toward which gift or gifts you may have. The spiritual gifts test in this study is based on honest introspection. It is designed to get you thinking about your spiritual life and looking intently at your own heart. The more sincere you are in your answers the more accurate the test results will be.

Spend some time now and complete the spiritual gifts test provided in **Appendix B**. Answer each question based on your actual behaviors and tendencies, not merely on what you believe or would like to be true about yourself. You may believe the truthfulness of the statement wholeheartedly, but your actions may not completely be aligned with that truth. Again, the more honest you are, the more accurate the results will be.

Once you have the results of your spiritual gifts test, bring them to a trusted friend or leader in your church family and ask them to give you feedback. Ask them to tell you where they see you serving in the body of Christ. Often other people can see things in us that we do not see ourselves. The Lord gives wisdom and insight to others in order to guide and encourage us in our walk with Him.

All Christians are a part of the "body of Christ." A body is a great analogy of how we are to be joined together as a church. Think of your own body and all of the parts that are necessary for the daily functions of life. How difficult would it be to lose an eye or a finger or a foot? Some of you reading this may have already experienced this or know someone who has. Of course, people are able to adjust and live without some parts, but life is much more difficult that way.

Read 1 Corinthians 12:12-31

According to verses 12-13, who is it that bonds the body together?

Some Christians do not feel as if they have a significant place in the church. In verses 15-20, what does Paul say about how we view ourselves in the body? Why is diversity in the body of Christ so important?

According to verses 21-26, how are we to view the other parts of the body? Why?

Some of us are worried that we will not live up to what others in the body are doing with their gifts. We like to compare ourselves to others and forget that we are an important part of the body, and we are called to connect and contribute according to how God has called and gifted us. You don't have to look pretty when serving in the body of Christ. In fact, you may never look pretty, but that doesn't take away the fact that you are an integral part of the life and ministry of the church.

My big toe is ugly. Actually, all of my toes are ugly, but I am glad I have all 10 of them! And ears are just plain weird looking. Right? But aren't we all glad we have them? The point is that we can serve without being refined or polished. We can serve in our weakness and *odd-shapedness* and still glorify God and build up His church. Don't be afraid to start serving Him because you aren't as capable as the next person. God has gifted you according to how He has made you so just be faithful in that.

Read Matthew 25:14-30

One of the greatest things in this passage is that the reward of the servant with two talents was the same as the servant with five talents. "Well done, good and faithful servant. You have been faithful over a little; I will set you over much. Enter into the joy of your master." They both were invited to enter into the joy of their master. Isn't that what we all want to hear? Their reward was not based on amounts of profit, but on their faithfulness with what they had been given. This is how The Lord deals with us. He is pleased with faith and faithfulness.

So how will you know that you are gifted in a certain way? Well, you will know when you begin to serve. Simply put, The Lord will confirm it in your heart by giving you joy and power and fruitfulness when you are faithfully serving in your gift. You will not be burdened by serving but will actually receive great enjoyment and happiness when you serve. You will have a strong desire to serve in that way because of the blessings it brings to your heart. And you will grow in your gift and get better at it. It may seem strange but this is how God will prove your gift to you.

The Lord is good and He wants you to know and serve in your gift. So the next thing to do is just that: serve Him in the local church body and get involved in what God is doing here and now. You won't be disappointed.

Questions for Group Discussion

Share with your group what you discovered about yourself this week. What spiritual gift do you have? Was this discovery surprising? How has The Lord confirmed this to you?

When reading the spiritual gift definitions in Appendix A, what gift or gifts stood out to you? How accurate were they in describing your giftedness?

If you could have any spiritual gift other than the one you have, what would it be? Why?

It is incorrect to think of spiritual gifts as merely personal gifts from God which are primarily for our own benefit and growth. They are given to the individual but within the context of the body of Christ, the church. Why is it important to keep this perspective when serving in our spiritual gifts?

What is the most difficult thing about being connected in the church like a body? What are the greatest blessings?

Why is it necessary to not compare ourselves to others in the church? What is the most important thing to The Lord in our serving Him?

What is the greatest reward for our faithful service to God?

LESSON 7: SERVE IN YOUR SPIRITUAL GIFT

You're going to fail. Yep, it's true. You are inevitably going to blow it big-time. I say this because it happened to me. Again and again actually, and unfortunately it will probably continue to happen. Now, we don't want to have a fatalistic or pessimistic attitude, but this is the reality of the battle we face each day in our walk with Jesus. We fail because we are in the battle, which is a good thing, but we also fail because we struggle against sin and fear and the lies of the enemy. We already know The Lord gives us perfect gifts, but we are still imperfect and we can mess things up, or simply fail to use our gifts when prompted by the Holy Spirit. The battle is not meant to wear us out, but to mold us and strengthen our hearts when we come through it.

You will fail, but you are also going to succeed because you will refuse to give up! How do I know this? Because the Spirit of God dwells in all who have faith in Jesus. And because Jesus has prayed for us and continues to intercede on our behalf each moment of our lives.

He doesn't pray that we would avoid the battlefield or its countless perils, but that our faith would endure to the end.

Read the following passages:

Luke 22:31-32
John 17:15-21

What is the result of Peter's endurance through failures and trials in Luke 22:32?

Why is this important to Jesus and His church?

Jesus knew Peter would fail (Luke 22:33-34) but He also knew Peter would eventually have his faith proven and strengthened. What assurance does this give you knowing that Jesus loves you in the same way He loved Peter?

In John 17 Jesus prayed for us. He prayed that we would be kept in the Father and that we would have unity in The Father and The Son. What was the reason He gave in verse 22? How does this link to the purpose of the Holy Spirit and spiritual gifts?

Sure we will sometimes fail, but how can we minimize our potential for failure? One way is to be aware of the likely hazards we will face as active members of the body of Christ. If we know those hazards ahead of time, we can plan on how we will react when faced with them in the midst of battle.

One of the reasons we fail in using our gifts is that we don't connect them in our hearts with the mission Jesus has for us. The Great Commission is the command of Jesus to His church. Having all authority, He told His disciples that they were to make new disciples, baptizing them in the name of the Father and of the Son and of the Holy Spirit, teaching them to observe all that He had commanded. We share this mission as devoted followers of Jesus.

He has given us gifts to fulfill our part in the Great Commission within the context of the church body. It is vital to continually remind ourselves of the connection between spiritual gifts and our mission together. This is why we identified the purpose of spiritual gifts in lesson five as *glorifying Jesus by testifying of Him to the world and building up His church.* Keeping this perspective will help us avoid idleness, laziness and indifference.

Read the following verses

1 Thessalonians 5:19
1 Timothy 4:14
2 Timothy 1:6

These verses remind us that we have hearts that need to be constantly brought under the lordship of the Holy Spirit. Our bent is to quench, deny, push against and be deaf toward His leading in our lives. "Do not quench the Holy Spirit" means not to extinguish the gift that is in you by rejecting the leading of the Holy Spirit. It means not to waste opportunities to be used by Him in daily ministry, and not to neglect the gifts which have been given to you, but instead to use them and grow in them each day.

Read 1 Corinthians 12:27-13:3

We can fail when we do not connect our gifts to our mission, but we can also fail when we do not use them in love. The way to serve Jesus in our gifts is the way Jesus served the world, which is in love.

All of the giftedness and power in the world is meaningless and empty if you lack love for God and for your neighbor. Love is to be the fuel for our actions in Jesus. And how do we love like Jesus? We abide in Him and in His love.

Take a few moments to read 1 John 4:7-21

This is a powerful passage of Scripture. Based on verses 9-11, what should be our motivation for loving others?

How can we know that we are abiding in The Lord? (See verses 13-16)

What is the point John makes in verses 20-21? Why is this important?

We love with a heart of gratitude. We love because God first loved us. In essence, His love enables our love, both for Him and for our neighbor. God showed us the greatest love by sending His Son. Jesus showed the greatest love by willingly dying for us on the cross. The Holy Spirit shows us the greatest love by dwelling with us and in us. This is how we can know that God is love: He has shown us love and He has proven that He is love.

Our response to God's love is to serve Him in our gifts, by faith, in love and humility.

Read Philippians 2:1-11

We see in this passage the principles of unity, love, selflessness, humility, and obedience. Our God and Savior Jesus Christ modeled these perfectly and expressed them fully throughout His life and ministry on earth. He is our Great Example and the One who we are to become more like each day.

If you call Jesus Lord and Savior, then you have a mission. You have work to do that He has prepared in advance for you to accomplish. In this study we have learned and discovered many important truths about God and about ourselves. There has been a lot of head work and heart work. Now is the time for foot work.

Idleness, laziness and indifference are three very powerful enemies of ours. But there is one greater: fear. Fear of rejection. Fear of embarrassment. Fear of exposing our weakness. Fear of the opinions of others. Fear of loss. Fear of the unknown. Fear of failure. Even fear of success. These all have the potential to grip us to the core. But The Lord is with us and He is for us. Jesus promised He will never leave us or forsake us. Our eyes must be fixed on Him for the journey, and His perfect love for us will overcome all of our fears.

God has given us His Spirit to gift us and guide us and empower our daily walk. He has prepared a special ministry for each of us to complete. Remember we have all we need, right now. All we need to do is take that first step. An incredible journey of faith awaits each of us.

Questions for Group Discussion

What are some of the potential pitfalls you might face while serving in your gifts? What are some proactive ways you can avoid them?

Jesus knows us better than we know ourselves. He knows when we will fail and when we will succeed. How is this encouraging or challenging to you?

Why is it important to connect our giftedness to our mission? How can we make sure to keep the right perspective while serving The Lord in our gifts?

Why do you think the Bible warns us to "not quench the Holy Spirit?" Can you identify a time where you did just that? What was the result? What would you do differently if faced with that situation now?

God has prepared a special ministry for each of us to complete. What work or ministry do you think He has prepared for you to do? What are the next steps you will take to begin that work? What might be some of the challenges you will face?

Fear is a powerful emotion. It can motivate or paralyze. What do you fear the most in serving God?

Looking back at this entire study, what do you think was the most important thing you learned? How will that lesson change the way you live for Christ?

SPIRITUAL GIFT DEFINITIONS

Administration

The Greek word for the spiritual gift of administration is *kubernesis*. This is a unique term that refers to a shipmaster or captain. The literal meaning is "to steer," or "to rule or govern." It carries the idea of someone who guides and directs a group of people toward a goal or destination. We see variations of this word in verses like Acts 27:11 and Revelation 18:17.

With this gift the Holy Spirit enables certain Christians to organize, direct, and implement plans to lead others in the various ministries of the Church. This gift is closely related to the gift of leadership, but is more goal or task oriented and is also more concerned with details and organization. See also 1 Corinthians 12:28; Titus 1:4-5.

Apostleship

The spiritual gift of apostleship is sometimes confused with the office of Apostle. The office of Apostle was held by a limited number of men chosen by Jesus, including the twelve disciples (Mark 3:13-19) and Paul (Romans 1:1). The requirements for the office of Apostle included being a faithful eyewitness of Jesus' ministry and His resurrection (Acts 1:21-22; 1 Corinthians 9:1), and being called by Jesus

Himself (Galatians 1:1). The Apostles were given authority by Jesus to do many different things to establish the church, including writing Scripture and performing miracles (John 14:26; 2 Peter 3:15-16; 2 Corinthians 12:12).

There are no more who hold the office of Apostle today, but the gift of apostleship continues in a different sense. Jesus gave apostles, along with prophets, evangelists, shepherds and teachers at His ascension (Ephesians 4:7-12). These represent a distinct category of apostles. They do not have the authority to write Scripture as the original Apostles did. They also have a different purpose in the sense of establishing the church – the foundation has already been set.

The Greek word for apostle is *apostolos* meaning a delegate or representative who is sent with a message and a mission. The message of those with the gift of apostleship today is, of course, the gospel. The mission is to plant new ministries and churches, go into places where the gospel is not preached, reach across cultures to establish churches in challenging environments, raise up and develop leaders, call out and lead pastors and shepherds, and much more. They often have many different gifts that allow them to fulfill their ministry. These are leaders of leaders and ministers of ministers. They are influencers. They are typically entrepreneurial and are able to take risks and perform difficult tasks. Missionaries, church planters, certain Christian scholars and institutional leaders, and those leading multiple ministries or churches often have the gift of apostleship. See also Ephesians 4:11; 1 Corinthians 9:1; 12:28; Acts 1:21-22.

Discernment

The spiritual gift of discernment is also known as the gift of "discernment of spirits" or "distinguishing between spirits." The Greek word for the gift of discernment is *diakrisis*. The word describes being able to distinguish, discern, judge or appraise a person, statement, situation, or environment. In the New Testament it describes the ability to distinguish between spirits as in 1 Corinthians 12:10, and to discern good and evil as in Hebrews 5:14.

The Holy Spirit gives the gift of discernment to enable certain Christians to clearly recognize and distinguish between the influence of God, Satan, the world, and the flesh in a given situation. The church needs those with this gift to warn believers in times of danger or keep them from being led astray by false teaching. See also 1 Corinthians 12:10; Acts 5:3-6; 16:16-18; 1 John 4:1.

Evangelism

All Christians are called to evangelize and reach out to the lost with the gospel (Matthew 28:18-20), but some are given an extra measure of faith and effectiveness in this area. The spiritual gift of evangelism is found in Ephesians 4:11-12 where Paul says that Jesus "gave the apostles, the prophets, the evangelists, the shepherds and teachers, to equip the saints for the work of ministry, for building up the body of Christ." The Greek word for evangelists is *euaggelistes* which means "one who brings good news." This word is only found two other places in the New Testament: Acts 21:8 and 2 Timothy 4:5.

Evangelists are given the unique ability by the Holy Spirit to clearly and effectively communicate the gospel of Jesus Christ to others. They are burdened in their hearts for the lost and will go out of their way to share the truth with them. Evangelists are able to overcome the normal fear of rejection and engage non-believers in meaningful conversations about Jesus. Their gift allows them to communicate with all types of people and therefore they receive a greater response to the message of salvation through Jesus Christ. They continually seek out relationships with those who don't know Jesus and are open to the leading of the Holy Spirit to approach different people. They love giving free treasure away for Jesus (2 Corinthians 4:7), and it brings them great joy knowing that the "feet that bring good news" are beautiful to those who believe (Isaiah 52:7). See also Ephesians 4:11; Acts 8:5-12, 26-40; 21:8; Matthew 28:18-20.

Exhortation

The spiritual gift of exhortation is often called the "gift of encouragement." The Greek word for this gift is *parakaleo*. It means to beseech, exhort, call upon, to encourage and to strengthen. The primary means of exhortation is to remind the hearer of the powerful and amazing work of God in Christ, particularly in regard to the saving work of Jesus in the atonement. We see Paul commanding Titus to use this gift in Titus 1:9 and throughout chapter 2, particularly Titus 2:11-15. He similarly charged Timothy in 2 Timothy 4:2.

The Spirit of God gives this gift to people in the church to strengthen and encourage those who are wavering in their faith. Those with the gift of exhortation can uplift and motivate others as well as challenge and rebuke them in order to foster spiritual growth and action. The goal of the encourager is to see everyone in the church continually building up the body of Christ and glorifying God. See also Romans 12:8; Acts 11:23-24; 14:21-22; 15:32.

Faith

The spiritual gift of faith is not to be confused with saving faith. All Christians have been given saving faith (Ephesians 2:8-9), but not all receive this special gift of faith. The word for faith in the New Testament is *pistis*. It carries the notion of confidence, certainty, trust, and assurance in the object of faith. The gift of faith is rooted in one's saving faith in Christ and the trust that comes through a close relationship with the

Savior. Those with this gift have a trust and confidence in God that allows them to live boldly for Him and manifest that faith in mighty ways.

In the Bible the gift of faith is often accompanied by great works of faith. In Acts 3:1-10 we see this gift in action when Peter sees a lame man at the Beautiful Gate and calls on him to stand up and walk in the Name of Jesus. Jesus said even a small amount of this faith could move mountains (Matthew 17:20; 21:21). Paul echoed this truth in 1 Corinthians 13:2.

The Holy Spirit distributes this gift to some in the church to encourage and build up the church in her confidence in God. Those with the gift of faith trust that God is sovereign and He is good. They take Him at His Word and put the full weight of their lives in His hands. They expect God to move and are not surprised when He answers a prayer or performs a miracle. See also 1 Corinthians 12:9; Hebrews 11:1-40.

Giving

The Greek word for the spiritual gift of giving is *metadidomi*. It simply means "to impart" or "to give." However, this word is accompanied in Romans 12:8 by another descriptive word: *haplotes*. This word tells us much more about the kind of giving that is associated with this gift. The word *haplotes* means "sincerely, generously and without pretense or hypocrisy."

The Holy Spirit imparts this gift to some in the church to meet the various needs of the church and its ministries, missionaries, or of people who do not have the means to provide fully for themselves. The goal is to encourage and provide, giving all credit to God's love and provision. Those with this gift love to share with others the overflow of blessings God has given them. They are typically very hospitable and will seek out ways and opportunities to help others. They are also excellent stewards and will often adjust their lifestyles in order to give more to the spread of the gospel and the care of the needy. They are grateful when someone shares a need with them, and are always joyful when they can meet that need. See also Romans 12:8, 13; 2 Corinthians 8:1-5; 9:6-15; Acts 4:32-37; Galatians 4:15; Philippians 4:10-18.

Healing

The spiritual gift of healing found in 1 Corinthians 12:9 is actually plural in the Greek. *Charismata iamaton* is literally translated "gifts of healings." This spiritual gift is closely related to the gifts of faith and miracles. All spiritual gifts are to be exercised in faith, but gifts of healings involve a special measure of it. This gift is interesting in that there is no guarantee that a person will always be able to heal anyone he or she desires. It is subject to the sovereign will of God, as all spiritual gifts are.

The Disciples were given authority to heal and cast out demons, but they were not always successful. The Apostle Paul was not able to heal himself and was told that God's grace was sufficient to carry him through his infirmity without removing it from him (2 Corinthians 12:7-10). This gift is given at various times and places to reveal the God of heaven to the sick and tormented. If healing is not granted, then we can conclude that God has greater plans for letting the person go through the illness or infirmity.

The spiritual gift of healing is an intimate one as it reveals the heart and compassion of God. Jesus is the Great Healer and Physician and during His ministry on earth He healed countless people and cast out demons (Matthew 4:23-24; 8:16; 9:35; Mark 1:34). Healings reveal that God is near to His people and He cares about their sufferings. Healings are meant to draw people to God through His Son Jesus Christ.

God wants those healed to respond in faith with thanksgiving and love as the leper did in Luke 17:15-19, and as the demon-possessed man did in Mark 5:18-20. By God's grace, physical healing should lead to spiritual healing (faith in Jesus) and eternal life with Him in heaven.

Those who have this gift are compassionate toward the sick and pray over them regularly. They have great faith and trust that God can and will heal some and are not deterred when He chooses not to. They are motivated knowing that God's revealed power will draw people to faith in Jesus. Their ultimate concern is the spiritual well-being of those being healed and their relationship with Jesus. They yearn for the day that there will be no more pain and suffering, and sin will no longer wreak havoc on the people of God. See also 1 Corinthians 12:9, 28, 30; James 5:13-16.

Interpretation of Tongues

The spiritual gift of interpretation of tongues is found alongside the gift of speaking in tongues in 1 Corinthians 12:10. The Greek word for interpretation is *hermeneia* and simply means to interpret, explain, or expound some message that is not able to be understood in a natural way. Thus, this spiritual gift is the supernatural ability to understand and explain messages uttered in an unknown language.

This is a revelatory gift, meaning that God "reveals" the meaning of the words or message being spoken and allows the interpreter to communicate its meaning to those who need to hear it. When this gift is exercised in the church two things happen: the church is edified and God is glorified.

The spiritual gift of interpretation is given by the Holy Spirit to certain individuals to reveal messages spoken in an unknown tongue to God for the building up of the church. Like the gift of prophecy, tongues that are interpreted have the effect of encouraging and blessing the church to love and serve God more deeply and effectively. See also 1 Corinthians 12:10, 30; 14:1-28.

Knowledge

The spiritual gift of knowledge is also known as the "word of knowledge" or "utterance of knowledge." The Greek word for this gift is *gnosis* and it simply means knowledge and understanding. The Scriptural emphasis in 1 Corinthians 12:8 is on the ability to speak this knowledge to others in a given situation. In the opening passages of 1 Corinthians, Paul spoke of knowledge and recognized that the highest form of knowledge among men is the gospel of Jesus Christ (i.e. the testimony about Christ, cf. 1 Corinthians 1:4-7). What we can conclude then is the gift of knowledge is an understanding of the things in this world and in our lives that is founded in the gospel and rooted in the Scriptures. This gift is closely related to the gift of wisdom which is alluded to by Paul in 1 Corinthians 1:18-31.

The Holy Spirit gives this spiritual gift to some believers to bring about understanding and to inform the church or individual believers. The person with this gift is usually well-versed in the Scriptures and often has much committed to memory. They can retain the truth and communicate it effectively at the appropriate times. The gift of knowledge allows a believer to relate the Scriptures, and particularly the gospel of Jesus Christ, to all aspects of life in this world. They can see how it connects to every situation and circumstance and how the reality and truth of the gospel is to inform every decision a Christian makes. See also 1 Corinthians 12:8; Romans 15:14; 2 Corinthians 2:14.

Leadership

The spiritual gift of leadership is closely related to the gift of administration and, interestingly, the spiritual gift of pastor/shepherd. The Greek word for the spiritual gift of leadership is *proistemi.* This word means to lead, to assist, to protect and to care for others. The spiritual gift of leadership is found in Romans 12:8 sandwiched between the gifts of giving and of mercy. It is placed there intentionally to show that it is a gift associated with caring for others. This is what connects it to the gift of pastor/shepherd, and what differentiates it from the gift of administration. It is more people oriented than task oriented in its application. This is not to say those with the gift of administration do not care for people, of course they do, but those with the spiritual gift of leadership focus on people and relationships more directly.

The word *proistemi* is connected to caring for people in other passages as well. In 1 Thessalonians 5:12-13 Paul says to "respect those who labor among you and are over (*proistemi*) you in the Lord and admonish you, and to esteem them very highly in love because of their work." The labor and work of those who were leading the believers in Thessalonica was that of tirelessly caring for their souls. Paul also connects leadership to caring for others when he asks, "If someone does not know how to manage (*proistemi*) his own household, how will he care for God's church?" (1 Timothy 3:5)

The Holy Spirit gives the spiritual gift of leadership to some in the church to care for God's people and lead them into deeper relationship with Christ and each other. They base their success on how well they help others succeed and grow in their spiritual walk with Jesus. They are able to accomplish many different tasks and objectives as they lead, but they will always lead relationally and with a deep concern for the well-being of others. They are "visionary" and less concerned with mundane details than those with the spiritual gift of administration. Many are entrepreneurial and willing to take risks to see the kingdom of God advanced through the church. They will go to great lengths to protect those under their care and are well-equipped to lead through crisis situations. See also Romans 12:8; 1 Thessalonians 5:12; 1 Timothy 3:4-5, 12; 5:17.

Mercy

All Christians are called to be merciful because God has been merciful to us (Matthew 18:33; Ephesians 2:4-6). The Greek word for the spiritual gift of mercy is *eleeo.* It means to be patient and compassionate toward those who are suffering or afflicted. The concern for the physical as well as spiritual need of those who are hurting is covered by the gift of mercy. Those with this gift have great empathy for others in their trials and sufferings. They are able to come alongside people over extended periods of time and see them through their healing process. They are truly and literally the hands and feet of God to the afflicted.

The Holy Spirit gives the spiritual gift of mercy to some in the church to love and assist those who are suffering, and walk with them until The Lord allows their burden to be lifted. The gift of mercy is founded in God's mercy towards us as sinners and is consistently expressed with measurable compassion. Those with this gift are able to "weep with those who weep" (Romans 12:15) and "bear one another's burdens" (Galatians 6:2). They are sensitive to the feelings and circumstances of others and can quickly discern when someone is not doing well. They are typically good listeners and feel the need to simply "be there" for others. See also Romans 12:8; Matthew 5:7; Luke 10:30-37; James 3:17; Jude 22-23.

Miracles

The spiritual gift of miracles is described in Scripture much like the gift of healing. It is found in 1 Corinthians 12:10 and the Greek phrase *energemata dynameon* literally translates "workings of powers." The double plural most likely means that these gifts were diverse and were not permanently available at the will of the gifted believer, but instead were bestowed at various times and circumstances. Thus, the gifts are subject to the divine will and purposes of God and are not decided by the one who performs the miraculous works.

We know that Jesus performed many miracles in His earthly ministry, even more than those recorded in Scripture (John 20:30-31, Acts 2:22). The Apostles regularly performed miracles of all kinds including casting out demons, healings, raising people from the dead, striking people dead, causing blindness, and much more (Acts 2:43; 3:1-10; 5:1-16; 9:36-43; 13:4-12; 19:11-12). Other believers performed miracles as well, including Stephen (Acts 6:8) and Phillip (Acts 8:4-8).

Miracles were given by God to the church to reveal the presence and glory of God among His people and to create a sense of awe and wonder and Godly fear. Though there were many enemies of the church, often the result of miracles being performed was more people coming to faith in Jesus and glorifying God, as well as greater faith and boldness within the church (Acts 4:29-31; 9:35, 42).

Those with the spiritual gift of miracles often have a heightened sensitivity to the presence and power of God through His Holy Spirit. They have a special measure of faith and desire for God to reveal Himself and draw many to faith in His Son Jesus Christ. They take care not to draw attention to themselves or have a following of people, but are constantly pointing others to Jesus. Those with this gift understand that God is Sovereign and He can work when and how He desires, but they make sure they are available and listening to the prompting of the Holy Spirit. This gift is often accompanied by prayer and strong petition by these individuals for God to reveal His glory to people. They do not claim power themselves, but always give credit and glory to God for His mighty works. Often God will deliberately humble them to keep them relying on His grace and pointing to His Son, rather than miracles. See also 1 Corinthians 12:10, 28-29; Acts 1:8; Galatians 3:5.

Pastor/Shepherd

The spiritual gift of pastor or shepherd is one that carries many different responsibilities. This gift is closely related to the spiritual gifts of leadership and teaching. The Greek word for pastor is *poimen* and simply means shepherd or overseer.

In the Biblical context, shepherds had several different responsibilities to their sheep and ultimately, to the owner of the sheep. They kept a lookout for predators and protected the sheep from attackers. They cared for wounded and sick sheep, nursing them back to health. They rescued them if they became lost or trapped. They spent enormous amounts of time with them guiding them to the places of nourishment and rest. The result was a trust and relationship that kept the sheep following the shepherd. The sheep were attuned to the shepherd's voice to the point that even if they were temporarily mixed with another herd, at the call of the shepherd they would separate and follow him.

Pastors are called shepherds because their calling and gifting are much like those who care for sheep. They are called and gifted to care for the spiritual well-being of a local body of God's people. Pastors are first and foremost servants. They are servants of God and servants of His bride, the church.

They are given a mixture of abilities by grace that allows them to serve the needs of an entire community.

The goal of the pastor is to reveal the glory of God in Christ by the power of the Holy Spirit to a people who need God's grace for life. The primary way the pastor will do this is by teaching the Word of God to the church. The gift of pastor is directly linked to the gift of teaching in Ephesians 4:11 and elsewhere. In fact, this gift could be called the gift of pastor-teacher. The ability to teach the Scriptures is also one of the many requirements of being an overseer (1 Timothy 3:1-7; Titus 1:6-9). By teaching the Scriptures to the church, the pastor feeds the "sheep" of God.

The Holy Spirit gives the spiritual gift of pastor to some in the church to humbly teach, guide, protect, and lead the church in the mission that God has for it, namely the Great Commission. The pastor loves the gospel of Jesus Christ and puts it at the center of his life and ministry. Pastors do not seek fame or recognition for themselves, but they are placed in a position of authority by the Holy Spirit. The role of a pastor is one of humility and service as he is reminded daily of his overwhelming need of God's grace for the task at hand. See also Ephesians 4:11; Jeremiah 3:15; Acts 20:28; John 10:11-18.

Prophecy

The spiritual gift of prophecy is an extraordinary and unique gift. Paul says in 1 Corinthians 14:1 to "Pursue love, and earnestly desire the spiritual gifts, especially that you may prophesy." This gift is a blessing to the church and should not be quenched or despised (1 Thessalonians 5:20). Those who have the gift of prophecy differ from the Old Testament Prophets who spoke the authoritative Word of God directly. Their words were recorded as Scripture as they proclaimed, "Thus says The Lord," whereas the messages from those with the spiritual gift of prophecy must be tested (1 Corinthians 14:29-33; 1 Thessalonians 5:20-21; 1 John 4:1-3). In the New Testament the Apostles, not the prophets, took over the role of Scriptural proclamation from the Old Testament Prophets.

The Greek word for the gift of prophecy is *propheteia* which is the ability to receive a divinely inspired message and deliver it to others in the church. These messages can take the form of exhortation, correction, disclosure of secret sins, prediction of future events, comfort, inspiration, or other revelations given to equip and edify the body of Christ (1 Corinthians 14:3-4, 24-25). Again, they do not constitute the authoritative Word of God, but are the human interpretation of the revelation that was received. They are spoken in human words through a human mind which is why they must be tested against the Scriptures (1 Thessalonians 5:20-21).

The Holy Spirit gives the gift of prophecy to some believers to make God's heart known and to edify the church. This gift is for the benefit of both believers and unbelievers and is a sign that God is truly among His church (1 Corinthians 14:22-25). Those with this gift are sensitive to both the prompting of the Holy Spirit and the needs of the church body. They should be humble and continually study the Scriptures in order to test these revelations before speaking them. When they do speak, they should allow and even expect others to weigh what is said against the Scriptures and interpret the message accordingly. In this way the church may be continually built up together in unity (1 Corinthians 14:4, 26). See also Romans 12:6; 1 Corinthians 12:10; 14:1-5; Ephesians 4:11-12; 1 Peter 4:10-11.

Serving/Ministering

The spiritual gift of service, or ministering, covers a wide range of activities in its application. There are two Greek words for this gift. The first one, found in Romans 12:7, is *diakonia.* The basic meaning of this word is "to wait tables," but it is most often translated in the Bible as "ministry." It refers to any act of service done in genuine love for the edification of the community. The word *antilepsis* is translated "helping" and is found in 1 Corinthians 12:28. It has a similar meaning: to help or aid in love within the community.

The Holy Spirit endows some believers with this gift to fill the many gaps of ministry and meet the needs of the church as it fulfills the Great Commission. The goal is to energize the church and free up others to use their gifts to the fullest. The result is the continued edification of the church and the added ability to see beyond its own needs and reach out into the community.

We see people with this gift in passages like Acts 6:1-7, 1 Corinthians 16:15-16, and many others. Those with the gift of service are committed to the spread of the gospel. They serve in ways that benefit others with different gifts and ministries that are more public. They have a heart devoted to Jesus and a desire to follow His command and example in Matthew 20:25-28 (cf. Mark 10:42-45).

Those with this gift do not seek recognition or a position in the "spotlight," they just love to help out. They are content with serving in the background knowing that their contribution will bless the church, display the love of Christ to the world, and bring glory to God. See also Romans 12:7; 1 Corinthians 12:4-7, 28; Acts 20:35; 2 Timothy 4:11; Revelation 2:19.

Teaching

The spiritual gift of teaching is one that carries a heavy responsibility in the church. In fact, James 3:1 warns, "Not many of you should become teachers, my brothers, for you know that we who teach will be judged with greater strictness." Like every believer, teachers are to be stewards of every word that comes out of their mouths. But the greater responsibility to which they are called is to be stewards of the Word of God to His people. Teachers have been entrusted with the task of explaining what the Bible says, what it means, and how we as followers of Jesus Christ are to apply it to our lives here and now.

The Greek word for those with the spiritual gift of teaching is *didaskalos*. From the root of this word we get our English word, "didactic." The word *didasko* means to teach, instruct, instill doctrine, explain, and expound. Those with the spiritual gift of teaching love to study the Word of God for extended periods of time. They consume the Scriptures as food for their hearts, souls and minds with the expressed purpose of knowing Him and then making Him known to others. They want to know what God has revealed of Himself and what He requires of us as people created in His image. They take great joy and satisfaction in seeing others learn and apply the truth of God's Word to their lives. They love to see how the gospel is woven throughout the Scriptures and how it glorifies and magnifies Jesus Christ in the hearts and lives of those who love Him by grace.

The Holy Spirit gives certain people the spiritual gift of teaching so that they would help the church fulfill her ministry as "a pillar and buttress of the truth" (1 Timothy 3:15). Without this gift, the church would quickly fall into error and sin. Teachers are there to make sure that doesn't happen. They hate when Scripture is abused and used out of context or with ill intent. They love the truth and speak the truth in love. They will never hide or withhold it. On the contrary, they desire to follow in the footsteps of Jesus who taught in the synagogues and in the Temple as well as anywhere the people were gathered. They are called to demonstrate God's love while revealing His truth to the world without fear. The effect of their ministry is the upholding of God's Word and the growth and maturity of His Bride until the day of His return. See also Ephesians 4:11; 1 Corinthians 12:28; Romans 12:7; James 3:1.

Tongues

The spiritual gift of tongues is more accurately called the gift of *languages.* The Greek word for tongues is *glossa*, which literally means "tongue." When it is used in the New Testament addressing the subject of spiritual gifts it carries the contextual meaning of "languages." Speaking in tongues is the utterance of prayer or of a message glorifying God, typically spoken to God, in a language that is unknown to the one speaking it.

To properly understand this gift, we need to begin with a brief history of language in the human race. In the garden mankind had one language and was in direct communication with God, having perfect communion with Him. Unfortunately, this relationship changed at the fall when Adam sinned against God and he and Eve were cursed and banished from Eden along with their descendants. Mankind continued to have one language up until Genesis 11 where God confused their language and people were dispersed throughout the earth. He did this because they had united together *in one language* and conspired to build a tower at Babel. Their intention was to "make a name" for themselves and thus replace God in their hearts. Pride is the birthplace of sin and regrettably fallen man has decided to use every advantage, including language, to usurp God's authority and place himself upon a throne which is not rightfully his.

After God confused their language and scattered them across the earth, He chose one people with one language to bring Him glory and draw mankind back to Himself. Abram, later called Abraham, was the one through whom God promised to bless "all the nations." Eventually, through the nation of

Israel, the Hebrew language would be used to communicate God's Word to the nations. However, the rest of the world did not speak or understand this language and for the most part continued to remain ignorant of God's plan of redemption.

Fast forward to Pentecost and the pouring out of the Holy Spirit on the people of God. Here we see a glimpse of God's reversal of the curse of divided languages. In Acts 2 people from all over the world hear God's people proclaiming His mighty works *in their own languages.* This is the beginning of the redemption of language for its intended purpose: to glorify God and draw all people to Himself.

In heaven an innumerable group from every nation, tribe, people and *tongue* will join together to praise God with *one language.* (See Revelation 7:9-12. This is where tongues will cease as mentioned in 1 Corinthians 13:8-10.) The intention of the spiritual gift of tongues is to glorify God now, but also to prepare ourselves as His church to glorify Him forever in heaven. The gift however is only partial, in that it is not given to all believers, and in the context of the church requires an interpreter in order for it to be edifying.

There is much more to be said about the spiritual gift of tongues, but we will summarize a few points here:

- Not every believer receives this gift. The gift of tongues is not a requirement or a necessary sign of salvation. See 1 Corinthians 12:30.
- Tongues can be human languages such as those heard in Acts 2, but often may be languages no one understands. See 1 Corinthians 14:2.

- Tongues are not "ecstatic speech" but are always orderly and are able to be controlled by the one speaking. See 1 Corinthians 14:27-28, 33, 39-40
- No tongues should be spoken in the church gathering without interpretation. See 1 Corinthians 14:27-28.
- Tongues should not be forbidden. See 1 Corinthians 14:39.

The Holy Spirit gives some believers the spiritual gift of tongues to glorify God and, with the help of an interpreter, to edify the church. This gift is dealt with extensively in the Scriptures and its use should be encouraged. That said, it should be used properly with pure motives and intentions, of course in the power and prompting of the Holy Spirit. See also 1 Corinthians 12:10, 30, 14:4, 39; Acts 2:4; 19:6.

Wisdom

The spiritual gift of wisdom, like the gift of knowledge, is also referred to as the "word of wisdom" or "utterance of wisdom." The Greek word for wisdom is *sophia* and it refers to the intimate understanding of God's Word and His commandments which results in holy and upright living. In the context of 1 Corinthians 12:8, it means to speak to the life of an individual or to a specific situation with great understanding and a righteous perspective, with the goal of guiding others toward a life of holiness and worship.

Several Scriptures reveal the true beauty and fruit of wisdom. Psalm 111:10 says: "The fear of the LORD is the beginning of wisdom; all those who practice it have a good understanding. His praise endures forever!" Wisdom begins with the fear of the LORD. It begins with knowing who God is and who we are in comparison to Him. That leads to understanding and then to practicing righteousness. A life of wisdom ultimately results in the praise of God.

James 3:17 says "the wisdom from above is first pure, then peaceable, gentle, open to reason, full of mercy and good fruits, impartial and sincere." This is undoubtedly a work of the Holy Spirit in the life of a believer. The highest wisdom is found in the cross of Christ, which is "folly to those who are perishing, but to us who are being saved it is the power of God." (1 Corinthians 1:18).

The Holy Spirit gives some the spiritual gift of wisdom to not only impart the truth and understanding to believers, but to invoke a response of holiness and worship lived out in the world and amongst God's people. Wisdom doesn't end with knowledge, but is expressed in transformed hearts and lives.

Those with the gift of wisdom have a deep understanding of the holiness of God and the lack of holiness in their own hearts. They can recognize this in others as well and have the compassion and boldness to share that truth with them. They are able to take from their own life experiences and share what God has taught them through those things. They can easily recognize where a decision or action may lead and can warn against those that may be harmful or unfruitful. They can often see through the confusion of a situation and can give direction that would help an individual or group obtain a God-glorifying goal. The church needs those with the spiritual gift of wisdom to guide her through uncertain or difficult times. See also 1 Corinthians 2:1-16; 12:8; Colossians 1:9-10; 2:1-3; James 3:13-18.

SPIRITUALGIFTSTEST.COM
ADULT SPIRITUAL GIFTS TEST

How to take this test:

Romans 12:3 says, "For by the grace given to me I say to everyone among you not to think of himself more highly than he ought to think, but to think with sober judgment, each according to the measure of faith that God has assigned."

For the best results answer each statement below according to who you are, not who you would like to be or think you ought to be. How true are these statements of you? What has been your experience? What do others tell you? To what degree do these statements reflect your usual tendencies? Each question is very important, so take the time to reflect on each one. Your score is calculated at the end of the test.

Respond to each statement according to the following 0-5 point scale:

0 = Never; Not true
1 = Rarely; Seldom true
2 = Some of the time; Occasionally true
3 = Half of the time; Usually true
4 = Most of the time; Consistently true
5 = All of the time; Always true

Begin:

1. _______ I am skilled at organizing people to accomplish many different tasks and objectives.

2. _______ I like to venture out and start new projects.

3. _______ I can easily determine whether a statement is true to Scripture or not.

4. _______ I can clearly and effectively communicate the gospel to others.

5. _______ I believe everyone needs encouragement in this life, and I love to give it.

6. _______ I live confidently knowing that God is intimately concerned and involved with my life.

7. _______ I live a simple lifestyle so that I can give a larger portion of my income to The Lord's work.

8. _______ People often ask me my perspective or interpretation of specific passages of Scripture.

9. _______ I have been told that I am a "dreamer."

10. _______ I have great empathy for those who are facing difficult life challenges.

11. _______ I am very protective of the spiritual well-being of others.

12. _______ At times God has given me a message for an individual or group and compelled me to speak it to them.

13. _______ I enjoy doing everyday tasks that support the various ministries of the church.

14. _______ I spend large amounts of time studying the Word of God knowing that my effort will make a difference in someone's life.

15. _______ I often have helpful insights into situations that have not been made clear to others.

16. _______ I can clearly see what needs to be done and implement a plan to make it happen.

17. _______ I am willing to take risks for the kingdom of God that others may not.

18. _______ I pay attention to what people say and how they say it, particularly those who teach.

19. _______ I feel a burden of compassion for those who are lost without Jesus.

20. _______ When people are discouraged, I remind them of the power and promises of God found in Scripture.

21. _______ I trust God completely to answer my prayers according to His perfect will.

22. _______ I consistently and joyfully give of my income, often more than a tithe.

23. _______ The Spirit has brought to my mind information that I have been able to use to minister to others effectively.

24. _______ I have a vision for my church or ministry and I know what needs to be done to accomplish it.

25. _______ I see the sick or needy as those who most need the love and comfort that Jesus offers.

26. _______ I love spending time nurturing and guiding others in their faith.

27. _______ There have been occasions that I have received a revelation from the Lord and spoken it to the church.

28. _______ I readily volunteer to help in church when I know it will fill a practical need.

29. _______ I effectively communicate the Bible in ways that influence and motivate others to learn more.

30. _______ I have learned through my experiences in life and can often guide others who are facing similar difficulties or challenges that I have had.

31. _______ I am good at delegating responsibility and trust others to "do their jobs."

32. _______ I can minister to people in different cultures effectively.

33. _______ I am a quick and accurate judge of character.

34. _______ I seek ways to build relationships with non-Christians so that The Lord will use me to share the gospel with them.

35. _______ I am compelled to challenge and inspire growth in those whose faith is stagnant.

36. _______ I know God will come through even if I don't see any possible solution to my problem.

37. _______ When I give it brings me great joy knowing that more people will be served and touched with the gospel.

38. _______ I study the Bible regularly in order to share truth with others in and outside the church.

39. _______ I am not afraid to take risks to advance the kingdom of God through my church or ministry.

40. _______ I care deeply about those who are hurting and want to help them navigate through their tough times.

41. _______ I desire to help the wounded and lost find healing and shelter in Jesus Christ.

42. _______ The Lord has spontaneously given me information about an individual that I felt obligated to confront them with in order to restore them to God.

43. _______ I like to be in the background and have no need of recognition for my service in the church.

44. _______ I am able to explain deep theological truths in ways that even a child can understand them.

45. _______ I often help people by offering Scriptural lessons and principles as solutions to life's various challenges.

46. _______ I like to create ways to make things run efficiently in my life and work.

47. _______ God has given me influence over several different ministries and/or churches.

48. _______ I can readily sense the enemy or a demonic influence in a situation.

49. _______ I love to memorize Scripture to share with those who don't know Jesus as their Savior.

50. _______ I am not afraid to challenge someone if I know it will foster spiritual growth and boldness in their life.

51. _______ I will boldly move forward in a situation if I sense God's calling and provision to do so.

52. _______ I believe I have been blessed financially so that I may be a blessing to the church and her mission to reach the lost and help the poor.

53. _______ I retain most of what I learn and can recall it quickly when the need arises.

54. _______ I can readily identify leaders and love to help them grow in their gifts and abilities.

55. _______ I love to see people through the storms of life and show them the compassion that Jesus did.

56. _______ I care about the church and do all I can to see it grow and be built up in love.

57. _______ God has put in my mind urgent matters that were otherwise unknown that I have announced to the church.

58. _______ I set aside time in my week to help those in need in my church and community.

59. _______ I hate it when someone uses Scripture out of context for their own purposes.

60. _______ I can see where a group or individual's decisions and actions will lead them, and I offer to guide them in the right direction.

61. _______ Details matter to me and I pay special attention to make sure things are done correctly.

62. _______ I am qualified and able to establish and lead a new church or ministry.

63. _______ I can often tell if someone is being deceitful or dishonest before it becomes apparent to others.

64. _______ I love to share what Christ has done in my life and how He has changed me.

65. _______ Others have told me that my words have compelled them to step out and grow in their faith.

66. _______ Even when times are tough, I trust God completely to comfort me and provide for my needs.

67. _______ Stewardship is an important discipline in my daily walk with Christ.

68. _______ I like to share the truth and insights God has shown me with others.

69. _______ People often look to me to lead a group or project.

70. _______ I have been known to "care too much" and help others in their time of need.

71. _______ I long to see each person in the church fulfilling the Great Commission.

72. _______ I have suddenly received a message from God specific to our congregation and shared it for the edification of the entire church.

73. _______ If I recognize a need in the church I simply fill it without being asked.

74. _______ I pay attention to the words people use because each one is significant and has meaning.

75. _______ It is humbling to me when someone asks for my guidance, so I take great care to help them.

76. _______ I manage my time wisely.

77. _______ I have a strong desire to raise up leaders and pastors who will equip the church.

78. _______ Things tend to be black or white to me; I see things as good or evil, right or wrong, true or false.

79. _______ I am not afraid to plead with people to believe that Christ died for their sin and to confess Him as Lord and Savior.

80. _______ When others are faced with difficult situations, I boldly tell them of the faithfulness of God towards His people.

81. _______ I don't often worry because of my confidence in God's ability and willingness to see me through every circumstance.

82. _______ I seek ways to help others financially and share the love of Christ with them.

83. _______ I am able to relate the truth and realities of the gospel to all aspects of life.

84. _______ I am not afraid to step up and take charge in a crisis situation.

85. _______ I seek out those who are deemed "lost causes" and aid them in restoring their lives.

86. _______ The gospel of Jesus Christ is the foundation of my life and ministry.

87. _______ Others have recognized that often God has spoken clearly and directly to them through a message I have shared.

88. _______ I believe there is eternal significance in performing mundane tasks and service.

89. _______ I love discovering how the gospel is woven throughout the entire Bible as I increasingly spend time in study.

90. _______ I can easily see which plan or strategy is the best one in a given circumstance.

91. _______ My desk or workspace is set up so I can access whatever I need quickly.

92. _______ Other pastors and leaders often come to me for help and guidance.

93. _______ Others have told me that my perceptions or judgments of people, situations, or statements have proved trustworthy.

94. _______ Most of my conversations with non-Christians lead to me speaking about my faith in Jesus.

95. _______ If a person or a group is stumbling or deviating from the life God has intended for them, I will speak up and press them to remember and return to joyful life in Christ.

96. _______ I consistently encourage others to trust God in everything.

97. _______ I give generously and without pretense to the ministry of God's people.

98. _______ I can usually recall a Scripture verse or passage that applies to a given situation.

99. _______ I am more "visionary" than detail oriented. I concentrate more on the big picture than the day-to-day particulars.

100. _______ Others have showed appreciation that I have comforted and ministered to them at a low point in their lives.

101. _______ I do not seek the "spotlight," but God has called me to shepherd His people.

102. _______ I am always listening for the Spirit of God and I am open to receiving whatever message He has for me to share.

103. _______ I find joy in being a helper and assisting others in their ministries.

104. _______ Often the Holy Spirit gives me just the right words to say when I am teaching an individual or group.

105. _______ I can often see through the confusion or conflict in a situation and provide a practical and Scriptural solution to it.

Scoring Directions:

Use the scoring matrix on the next page to determine your highest score for each gift. Write your score (from 0-5) for each question in the box with that question number. Add up each column and write your total scores above the corresponding **Gift Code**. Once you have done this you can check the key below to see what spiritual gift each Gift Code represents. The highest score for any gift is 35. The higher the score, the stronger you are in that spiritual gift based on your responses.

Gift Codes:

Ad = Administration
Ap = Apostleship
Di = Discernment
Ev = Evangelism
Ex = Exhortation
Fa = Faith
Gi = Giving
Kn = Knowledge
Le = Leadership
Me = Mercy
Pa = Pastor/Shepherd
Pr = Prophecy
Se = Serving/Ministering
Te = Teaching
Wi = Wisdom

APPENDIX B

	1	2	3	4	5	6	7	8	9	10	11	12	13	14	15
	16	17	18	19	20	21	22	23	24	25	26	27	28	29	30
	31	32	33	34	35	36	37	38	39	40	41	42	43	44	45
	46	47	48	49	50	51	52	53	54	55	56	57	58	59	60
	61	62	63	64	65	66	67	68	69	70	71	72	73	74	75
	76	77	78	79	80	81	82	83	84	85	86	87	88	89	90
	91	92	93	94	95	96	97	98	99	100	101	102	103	104	105
Total															
Gift Code	**Ad**	**Ap**	**Di**	**Ev**	**Ex**	**Fa**	**Gi**	**Kn**	**Le**	**Me**	**Pa**	**Pr**	**Se**	**Te**	**Wi**

ABOUT THE AUTHOR

Jeff Carver is an ordinary pastor and founder of SpiritualGiftsTest.com. Since 2003 he has been dedicated to helping Christians discover and use their spiritual gifts to the glory of God. A graduate of Liberty Theological Seminary, he is passionate about discipleship and developing practical resources for the church to fulfill the Great Commission. His personal blog and other resources can be found at JeffCarver.com. He currently resides in Southern California with his wife, Michelle.

Made in the USA
Monee, IL
22 January 2020

20665430R00062